In the Past

by Rachel Benjamin

capstone
classroom

Let's take a trip to learn about the past.

Bill clips a ram. Bill is quick.

Viv and Jill sew a quilt. It is big.

Kim dips candles. The wax is hot.

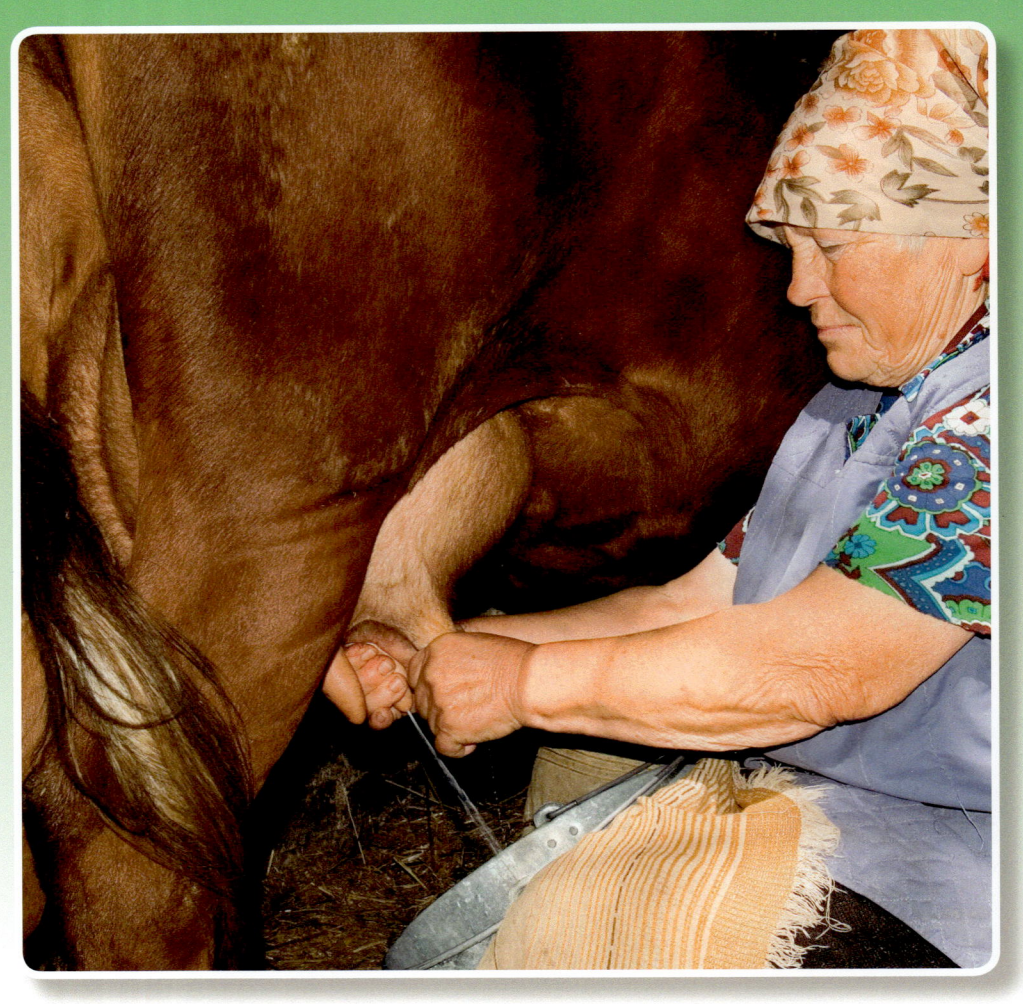

Lil milks a big cow. It will not kick.

Ron makes a horseshoe. Will it fit?

We went on a trip. What did we see?